M000164269

WARNING
TO
MINISTERS,
THEIR WIVES,
AND MISTRESSES

DR. BETTY R. PRICE

FAITH ONE
PUBLISHING

WARNING TO MINISTERS, THEIR WIVES, AND MISTRESSES
by Dr. Betty R. Price
Published by Faith One Publishing
7901 S. Vermont Avenue
Los Angeles, CA 90044

This book or parts thereof may not be reproduced in any form, stored in a retrieval system, or transmitted in any form by any means—electronic, mechanical, photocopy, recording, or otherwise—without prior written permission of the publisher, except as provided by United States of America copyright law.

This book is produced and distributed by Creation House, a part of Strang Communications, www.strangbookgroup.com.

Unless otherwise noted, all Scripture quotations are from the New King James Version of the Bible. Copyright © 1979, 1980, 1982 by Thomas Nelson, Inc., publishers. Used by permission.

Scripture quotations marked KJV are from the King James Version of the Bible.

Scripture quotations marked RSV are from the Revised Standard Version of the Bible. Copyright © 1946, 1952, 1971 by the Division of Christian Education of the National Council of the Churches of Christ in the USA. Used by permission.

Design Director: Bill Johnson
Cover design by Justin Evans

Copyright © 2009 by Dr. Betty R. Price
All rights reserved

Library of Congress Control Number: 2009926375
International Standard Book Number: 978-1-59979-774-8

10 11 12 13 — 9 8 7 6 5 4 3
Printed in the United States of America

Contents

FOREWORD

HAVING WORSHIPED IN CHURCH MY entire life, I must say I have seen and heard a lot. But what I think I am most amazed about is the large amount of scandal that sometimes takes place among those occupying the pulpit, particularly the kind of scandal that involves ministers. Most men of God will proudly tell you that they were in fact called by God to preach, but for whatever reason it seems that many of these ministers have sadly lost their way. It seems that some of them are no longer living according to God's Word and instead are living any way they see fit. They are doing whatever they want, whenever they want to, and are not paying much attention at all to the real plan God has set in place for them and His people.

Hence, it is because of all of the above that a few years ago, I sat down and wrote a novel that ultimately became a series about a pastor, his wife, and his mistresses. I wasn't sure how well this storyline would be received, but to my surprise, I began hearing from one reader after another, telling me that while my protagonist was fictional, he reminded them of their own pastors. What I heard, more often than not, was that it was about time someone wrote the truth about ministers and the affairs many of them are having—it was time someone wrote about what is really going on inside the church, without trying to sugarcoat it.

But today, I am here to tell you that my fictional stories have nothing on the real-life and very candid stories Dr. Betty Price so compassionately writes about in this life-changing work you are only minutes away from reading. This wonderful book is a most informative resource that should be read by every minister, regardless of whether he has just entered seminary or has been a pastor for decades. Additionally, it should be read by every minister's wife, including those who have faithful husbands and especially by those who are feeling the kind of pain and humiliation no wife should ever have to experience; and it should certainly be read by all mistresses, as well as by any woman who is even considering the idea of having an affair with a married minister.

Dr. Betty offers some truly remarkable advice, shares some of her own personal experiences, and skillfully backs up every single word with extremely powerful Scripture. So, as you embark on this very important reading journey, know that every page Dr. Betty has written is genuine, that her message comes straight from the heart, and that it will, without a doubt, help save many, many souls.

Dr. Betty Price is a true woman of God, a woman who loves and honors God to the fullest, and for that reason, it is my sincere joy and great pleasure to introduce to you *Warning to Ministers, Their Wives, and Mistresses.*

—KIMBERLA LAWSON ROBY
New York Times Best-selling Author

INTRODUCTION

I HAVE BEEN CONCERNED ABOUT MANY of the leaders of the body of Christ because of what I have seen in over fifty years of ministry with my husband. There are far too many people who live immoral lives, as if God were not real. I know of more true stories regarding adultery and immorality than I could possibly mention in this book. I know about stories of men who have had babies with various women in their churches, stories of perverted sex and minister husbands who have AIDS and STDs because they are sleeping with other men and then pass those diseases on to their wives; abominable things that God is not at all pleased with and that will provoke His wrath if not truly repented of.

I receive many calls from distraught wives telling me about the infidelity of their husbands. I even receive sad letters and calls from mistresses who have gotten involved with ministers and want to get out of the ungodly relationships. In many cases, the ministers threaten them or try to find ways to keep them in the relationship. After reading the two most recent correspondences of this type that were sent to me, my daughter Angela said, "Mom, you have to write your book." So I write it now on behalf of the thousands upon thousands of ministers who live right, and for the hopefully many, many young ministers who will read this book and avoid living unrighteous lives.

CHAPTER I

LETTERS FROM TWO MISTRESSES

THESE ARE THE CORRESPONDENCES I received that compelled me to write this book.

I just recently turned half a century. I'm so thankful to God for this blessing. So many women hide their age, but I'm thankful to see half a century gone by. I am writing to tell you that I'm a partner. I am not bragging about being a partner because I have not been faithful with my tithes or offerings and the commitment I made with Crenshaw Christian Center (CCC) in L.A.

I lost my job of ten years a couple of years ago...and I have not been able to find another one that has good benefits and one that's interesting while helping others...I was fired for wanting to be treated like the "Heathers" and "Brookes" that worked at the clerk office. I went back to school for a couple of semesters to bring myself up to date with modern computer technology.

Six months before my termination, the Lord

allowed me to purchase a three-bedroom, two-bath condo that's surrounded by lakes with people water skiing, fishing, and sailing their big boats. I was blessed to buy this condo while being faithful and obeying the Lord with paying tithes and offerings to CCC in Los Angeles, California. I sowed seeds into good, fertile soil with your ministry and was blessed with this purchase after filing bankruptcy and a foreclosure on my previous home.

Dr. Betty, I know I'm blessed because to this date, I have not missed one payment on any of my bills, including credit card purchases. Mind you, now, I was making ten dollars an hour working on a government job for ten years, with my starting salary of five dollars an hour. Granted, I don't live in a high life of luxury spending, but the life that I live is a life of trusting God for all my needs and for what His Word says—that if you have the faith of a mustard seed, you can move mountains out of your way. I was not sure what a mustard seed was [when I first heard that promise preached], so I went and purchased a box of them.

Anyway, I am writing because I can't seem to find my space here anymore at fifty. I'm going through my midlife feeling sorry for myself, gaining mad weight, and sitting around being lazy. I have started having an affair with a married man who happens to be an ordained bishop. I tell myself that everyone does it; then I ask the Lord to please forgive me, and

I try to move on with my life. But I keep going back on that "Lord, please forgive," and the forgiveness the Lord has extended to me many times. I can't seem to say no to the bishop's attention to me. And mind you, it's not a lot of attention that he is able to give to me. I used to talk—not really badly (but not nicely either)—about other women who engaged in adulterous relationships with other men.

Dr. Betty, I always prayed to the Lord not to ever let myself become involved with someone else's husband, especially a man of the Lord's cloth, because I feared the Lord and still fear Him. I pray and pray, but my self-esteem has been somewhat stripped by what happened at [work]. It's been two years, and [yet] I have all of this work experience and can't find a job at fifty years old.

Please pray for me, please!

Oftentimes I ask the bishop, Aren't you afraid of the Lord, or do you and He have just that tight understanding? He says that every time he leaves my presence, he feels really bad, but not bad enough to just stop. And get this, Dr. Betty, I had been without an intimate relationship with anyone for eight years and was trying to wait for the Lord to send me my husband, friend, and constant companion. I told the bishop this before we ever had a physical relationship. You would think that he would be thinking with his big head...

This is an extremely small amount of money to

send to say that I am so grateful...for your husband's teaching that I watch each week on Sundays. I used to send my tithes to CCC in Los Angeles...I've slacked off big time because I don't have a lot coming in, but I do have a little coming in.

Please keep me and others like me ('cause I'm not the only one in a sick situation like this; some folks are way far worse than mine) in your prayers. I also practice what Dr. Price Sr. says: "Learn to pray for yourself." I do and pray for others as well.

I mean not to bother you, for I know that folks write to you every day about such petty things. As I mentioned earlier, I turned one-half of a century this year, and I only celebrate the decades in my birthdays, like at thirty, forty, and now fifty. I thank God for [the numbers] one through nine, but after the first thirty years, they started coming too fast. I decided to just celebrate the decades in those years of life. I try to do something really special on that decade year, and writing to Dr. Betty Price is my really special something this decade. If I get a response that would be cool and the best of the best, but please let me assure you that I am so thankful for just being allowed to just write to her...

I know it sounds corny, but that's what I like...Please pray that I find the right job that the Lord might have for me so that I may help myself and others and not have such a low self-esteem...

Dr. Betty, I respect people's union with God,

because when the Lord blesses me with such a
union, I would want it also to be respected...

I have a very heavy heart as I write this e-mail, since
I do not know how to say what I am about to explain
to you.

I have been a Christian for more than eight
years... I was married for five years, and my marriage
should not have happened in the first place. We got
counseling from the pastor of our church, and it did
not work.

When I became separated from my husband, who
was a leader of the church and later left, my pastor
and prophet started an intimate relationship with
me. At first I was very hesitant, but what he said
made sense. And so, I fell in love. I now realize that
it was not love.

Due to this relationship, I blossomed in the
house of the Lord. I started many different things
and made lots of money for the church. I started
preaching and ministering in dance, so much so
that I minister at other churches. The power of
the Lord is so overwhelming that people receive
breakthroughs.

It has now been four years since the relationship
started, and I have become very antagonistic toward
him. I am disrespectful in major meetings and angry
all the time. During the four years we have been

together intimately I have not been faithful. I have always felt like this is not right, so I started other relationships to take away the pain of being with a married pastor, prophet, and motivational speaker with three kids.

He, the pastor, has always supported me, and if I need anything at all I can have it. But I am bitter, and it is manifesting in the way I behave.

I don't know why, but it is getting worse. Sometimes I feel like just dying. I have contemplated suicide more than once.

Recently—and this is why I need your advice and prayer—the pastor said that God told him I needed to change. I have always felt like God did not want this relationship, but he says that God wants us, me and him together in an intimate relationship, to grow his church. I suggested we change our relationship to friendship, since I felt this was probably what God wanted. He got angry, and I got scared. So, we are in a relationship still. He ended up saying that God wanted me to be a good girl and to stop giving him trouble. If I do what God wants, then all my ministries would come forth. Right now, he says I am hindering the work of the Lord by being this way to him.

I have also become quite unfired for the work that gave me so much joy and energy. Although, I still spend every evening after work in church, and I still show up to do whatever work I am asked to do.

I still have meetings with my volunteers, and things go as normal. But people are starting to notice the difference in me and in the way I treat the pastor.

I don't want to be this angry person, but I need release. I know in the Bible it says, "Believe in the Lord and you shall be established, believe in his prophet and you shall prosper" [2 Chron. 20:20]. I know that I should never question God, and the pastor hears from God and relays the message. I don't know what I am asking from you, but God will tell you how to answer me. I know.

Why am I coming to you? I had a vision of being in your church a long time ago. I believe what you and your husband preach with all my heart, and I know God will help me through you.

Please do not delay in a response. My life is at present hanging in a balance.

I thank you very much for your support.

My answer to the woman who wrote this e-mail was that her spirit was totally against the immoral lifestyle that she was sharing with the prophet. She needed to leave that ministry and repent, and God would forgive her.

> If we confess our sins, He is faithful and just to forgive us our sins and to cleanse us from all unrighteousness.
>
> —1 JOHN 1:9

> For I will be merciful to their unrighteousness, and
> their sins and their lawless deeds I will remember
> no more.
> —Hebrews 8:12

I also told her the scripture that she was referring to, 2 Chronicles 20:20, was talking about a righteous prophet, and if she did not get out of that situation, her future would not be good because there are consequences to the choices that we make. I talked with her again later, and at the time of that conversation she had not gotten out of the situation as yet because there are personal benefits that she is receiving from staying in it. My prayer for her is that the Holy Spirit will bring conviction to her to make the right decision before it is too late.

> This is a faithful saying: If a man desires the posi-
> tion of a bishop, he desires a good work. [God is
> telling you that this is a good work.] A bishop then
> must be blameless, the husband of one wife [not
> women on the side], temperate, sober-minded, of
> good behavior, hospitable, able to teach; not given
> to wine, not violent, not greedy for money, but
> gentle, not quarrelsome, not covetous; one who
> rules his own house well, having his children in
> submission with all reverence (for if a man does not
> know how to rule his own house, how will he take
> care of the church of God?); not a novice, lest being
> puffed up with pride he fall into the same condem-
> nation as the devil. Moreover he must have a good

> testimony among those who are outside, lest he fall
> into reproach and the snare of the devil.
>
> —1 TIMOTHY 3:1–7

Apparently a lot of ministers don't read this part of the Bible. They want to know about faith—how do I get a house, how do I get a car, how do I get clothes, or how do I get shoes? How about how to take care of your wife? Or wife, how about taking care of your husband? You need to learn how to use your faith for these types of things.

It says in Titus 1:5–9:

> For this reason I left you in Crete, that you should set in order the things that are lacking, and appoint elders in every city as I commanded you—if a man is blameless, the husband of one wife, having faithful children not accused of dissipation or insubordination. For a bishop must be blameless [*blameless* does not mean "perfect," but one against whom no evil can be proved; we are not perfect and might make mistakes], as a steward of God, not self-willed, not quick-tempered, not given to wine, not violent, not greedy for money, but hospitable, a lover of what is good, sober-minded, just, holy, self-controlled, holding fast the faithful word as he has been taught, that he may be able, by sound doctrine, both to exhort and convict those who contradict.

So I believe these are some things laid out for our leaders—pastors, men, and women in ministry.

CHAPTER 2

WARNING TO HUSBANDS

One Wife

LIKE I SAID BEFORE, THE Scripture does not say a pastor may have a woman on the side or women on the side. There is too much careless living among ministers of the gospel. My heart grieves because of this. I get many, many calls from pastor's wives from all over the country telling me about how their husbands are treating them. I don't know how in the world these men think they are going to please God or be blessed of God. If you are a pastor who is unfaithful to your wife and you feel that you are blessed, it is only going to be a temporary blessing; it is not going to be something that is lasting.

The pastor should be a faithful husband. Ephesians 5:25 tells husbands to love their wives as Christ loved the church, and Ephesians 5:33 tells the wives to reverence their husbands. In order to stay out of trouble, you should make rules for yourselves as a pastor and minister. We don't hear that much about women, but there are some women who get into adultery. They should apply the same guidelines and set boundaries for themselves. Pastors, you should have your wife help you in ministry. Some men don't want their wives to help them. They act like their marriages and ministry are separate and unrelated, like their wives are something out there and the ministry is something over here. Pastors, if you had your wife be a part of what you do, then you wouldn't be so prone to listen to the other sister or the secretary, who probably do not have your best interest at heart.

Too many ministers fall victim to infidelity and immoral living, and it grieves my spirit. If you love God, you should want to obey God. He said, "He who has My commandments and keeps them"—that means to obey them—"it is he who loves me" (John 14:21). Ephesians 5:25 says, "Love your wives, just as Christ also loved the church." Job wisely declared, "I have made a covenant with my eyes [if we make covenants with our eyes, we won't get in trouble]; Why then should I look upon a young woman? For what is the allotment of God from above, And the inheritance of the Almighty from on high? Is it not destruction for the wicked, And disaster for the workers of iniquity? Does He not see my ways, And count all my steps?" (Job 31:1–4). Job wasn't even born again, but he made some wonderful statements of wisdom that we as leaders could learn from.

CHAPTER 3

THE MANY FACES OF SEDUCTION AND DECEPTION

D O WE REALLY KNOW THAT God is real and that He is in our lives and with us in whatever we are doing? Apparently, many today don't realize this. Job was under the old covenant and even he knew it. Job 31:4 says, "Does He not see my ways, And count all my steps?" Do you know that God is with you when you are doing something you don't have any business doing? A pastor's wife should not have to get into a verbal or physical fight with any other woman of the church because of her husband's indiscretions, but I've heard stories of this happening. As a Christian woman, she should not have to lower herself to that level. Pastors, do you know what you do to your wife when you are unfaithful? They have such poor self-esteem when they are not treated the way they should be.

Pastors and ministers are in a position where they are surrounded by women, and women love pastors and men in leadership. But pastors need to know that they can't have all of the women who flirt with them and run after them, so they need to make some rules and boundaries for themselves because it's going to be one after another.

I spoke with a lady who told me that for twenty years her husband had been running around with women, one after another, in their church. She said that she didn't know it. She noticed different women missing from the congregation now and then, but did not have a clue as to why they were no longer around. But it caught up with him, and it will catch up with anyone who is living this lifestyle— including you, man of God. He had been running around all those years, and the only way she finally found out was that he became ill. He ended up having to tell her. Young ministers, learn this, because the temptations are going to come. This woman asked me what she should do, if she should stay with him. I informed her that she had biblical reasons to leave her husband when he is in adultery.

Infidelity is not always a reason to leave, but of course, only you can make that decision. If you decide to stay, then you are going to have to really forgive him—I mean really forgive him and purposely not remember all those things that he has done to you—because you will be worried and stressed out and cause sickness to come into your own body. And your body is the temple of the Holy Spirit. You have to think about all those things that are involved when you are in a situation like that. If you decide to stay, then you cannot hold anything against him. You would have to work that out personally by doing what Philippians 4:6 says: "Be anxious for nothing, but in everything by prayer and supplication, with thanksgiving, let your requests be made known to God." This means not to worry or be anxious for anything. Also, 1 Peter 5:7 says, "Casting all your care upon Him, for He cares for you."

Transformation is a p-r-o-c-e-s-s! Dr. Minnie Claiborne, minister and Christian counselor, provides steps to healing and deliverance in the final chapter of this book. You must make the decision to use your will, spend personal time with God, apply the Word of God, and, by faith in God, begin your journey to freedom one step and one day at a time. Being accountable to godly men and women is essential, and when necessary, seek good, professional Christian counseling. You will be eternally grateful that you did.

You Must Set Boundaries and Beware of "Traps"

There is far too much infidelity and careless living in the body of Christ. As I said earlier, leaders need to make rules and set boundaries for themselves. As a leader you are going to be approached by women and you will be tempted to approach women. You do not have to yield to the temptations. The Bible says to watch and pray that you enter not into temptation. The spirit indeed is willing but the flesh is weak. (See Matthew 26:41.) The devil will use anything and anyone to get you off course, especially if you are teaching the uncompromising Word of God, because you are a threat to him. You do not know where your ministry will take you and neither does the devil, but he will bring all kinds of temptations to you to try and get you to yield and veer off course.

In our earlier years when the ministry was just beginning to take off and we found out how to please God and were filled with the Holy Spirit, there was much excitement about the things of God.

> But without faith it is impossible to please Him, for he who comes to God must believe that He is, and that He is a rewarder of those who diligently seek Him.
>
> —HEBREWS 11:6

> And they were all filled with the Holy Spirit and began to speak with other tongues, as the Spirit gave them utterance.
>
> —ACTS 2:4

We had come through the hard times and struggles of the first seventeen years of our marriage. I knew how to be the wife that I needed to be and how not to withhold my body from my husband so that he was sexually satisfied and would not be interested in any other woman. But the devil tried to get to him another way. We had just gotten Spirit-filled and were hungry for the things of the Spirit. At that time there were many people giving prophecies and words from the Lord. During this time a young woman came to our ministry, and she was ever so spiritual. You have to be careful about these so-called spiritual women. She always had words for Apostle Price. She was telling him stuff all the time. She was at every church service, and every time a service was over she was right there in front of him. Nobody else could talk to him. She finally got our telephone number and started calling the house and continued telling him stories about what God was saying to her.

Men, you have to be very careful, because the devil can trick you. Even though you're not sexually involved, you can get your soul, mind, and emotions all messed up listening to such a person, mesmerizing you with all her stories about what God is doing and going to do in her life supernaturally.

Now, I know myself; I don't have any jealousy in me, but this woman's behavior was a little inordinate. It was beyond regular Christian love. My husband could not see it at the time because he was not interested in her sexually, but I could see that she was going to trap him another way. Because I could see the error in what she was doing, Apostle Price and I would be at odds with one another. I would tell him about it, and then he would get upset with me. The enemy could have used this situation because my husband would find her to talk with, which did not look right. You must keep in mind that the Bible says in 1 Thessalonians 5:22, "Abstain from every form of evil." She would tell him things, and it probably sounded interesting. She would say, "Well, I don't have anybody to talk to spiritually, and I need you." Then he, the apostle, would feel obligated and say, "I have to help this woman spiritually." I said, "No you don't. If God called her, let Him help her."

She had all these stories, and they were wonderful stories. See, I knew it wasn't God. The devil was trying to trap him. She told him, "You know, I see myself as the first black Kathryn Kuhlman. I see myself on stage; God has shown me this." Kathryn Kuhlman has died and gone to heaven, and that woman is not a black Kathryn Kuhlman yet—and that was thirty-eight years ago. But you see, the devil was giving her all of these stories to feed his interest in and desire for the supernatural. That was another way that Satan was trying to get him off track, listening to the wrong spirit, which sounded so good. He just could not see that this was wrong because he wasn't in adultery. But this woman was feeding his mind continually with her so-called words from God, and it was getting his soulish area all messed up emotionally because he liked hearing these stories she said were from God.

Well, it got so bad that I told him, "If you have to keep talking to this woman, then I am not going to church with you anymore." I am not like so many pastor's wives who pretend that all is well, and they are absolutely miserable. They ride to church every Sunday, fussing all the way there, and then get out of the car smiling and acting like everything is all right. I can't do that. I don't live like that. I told Fred, "If you must have this relationship, then I am not going to church with you another Sunday." I did miss a Sunday one time. He said, "If you wanted to hurt me, you really did." I said I was not going until that relationship ceased. He asked, "Well, what will you tell the people?" I said, "I'll just tell them that you are in a relationship with this person that is inappropriate, and it bothers me. If you can't change, then I'm going to step aside, because I know this relationship is destructive."

Satan was trying to trap him just before this awesome ministry took off. That woman had this thing so well planned that she had her little cohorts around helping her out. She had this one friend of hers give Apostle Price a so-called prophecy, saying, "My son, the time you are spending with sister so-and-so is of me." My husband was so innocent. He would show me everything that they gave him and tell me what she said God said. I said, "I don't care, because that is not God!" Then they started telling him about me, "Oh, she is just going through the change." I was thirty-eight years old at that time and had young Fred after that. I kept telling Apostle Price, "I don't care what they or you think is causing me to act this way; just stop it, because if you don't, I will not be around! So call it jealousy, call it going through the change, or whatever you want. I know my own heart, and I know that I am not jealous." I knew I was not going through the change at that time. I had to be really strong at that time and truly have a relationship with Jesus Christ, or I could have been wiped out, as so many pastor's wives are. So pastors and wives of pastors, recognize these kinds of relationships, and head them off at the pass before they evolve into something destructive.

So many women will not stand up for themselves when they see things that their husbands are doing that's not right, whether innocently or purposely. If you are married to a man who is behaving inappropriately, you need to say something, because you are his helpmate.

Sometimes women come into the church and interrupt—whether intentionally or innocently—what God has done through the pastor and his wife and where the ministry is flourishing. A so-called super-spiritual woman comes in and causes the minister or pastor to think that she can help him get to another level, and suddenly he thinks that he doesn't have anything in common with his wife anymore. This happened to a couple that used to come to our ministerial fellowship regularly. I watched the pastor being taken over by this supposedly highly spiritual woman, and tragically, he ended up leaving his wife and children. That is a satanic trap! For this reason, pastors, check your hearts.

Praise God, my husband and I got through that episode. He thanked me for taking a stand, even though he thought it was a good, spiritual relationship. Pastors, you do not need any close spiritual relationship with any woman. From that time until now, we have had no problems, and that was thirty-eight years ago. My husband changed, because he always wants to be right with God. God was getting him ready for this awesome ministry and Satan, through that woman, was trying to stop him.

CHAPTER 4

WHEN YOU LOSE YOUR ANOINTING AND YOUR POSITION, THEY WILL NO LONGER WANT YOU

A GREAT NUMBER OF MINISTER'S WIVES are facing extremely difficult situations. Some are facing situations in which their husbands enjoy flirting with women. Many actually have affairs, and children are born as a result of the affairs. Many wives try to hide the fact that their husband is unfaithful, and that is not good. When you try to hide the truth, it will eventually be revealed, and by then you've ended up hurting a lot more people. Ladies, I am not saying that if he made an unwise choice in committing adultery you should run and tell somebody. However, if he continues in that lifestyle after you've talked to him about it, then you should speak up in order to arrest his attention. The Bible says in Numbers 32:23, "Be sure your sin will find you out."

There is too much immoral living in the body of Christ. Sometimes as a wife you might say, "Well, if I tell someone, it may cost him his job as a pastor," or, "It's too embarrassing." You do not need to have all your trust in a man, even if it is your husband. If he is doing wrong, you need to stand for righteousness. You ought to love God more than you love that man. I'm not saying, "Don't love your husband." Standing up for right is loving your husband, because if he listens, it will save him from the wrath of God.

We have all had temptations, trials, and tests—things that we've had to face and say no to—so that unholy flesh needs to be crucified.

> I beseech you therefore, brethren, by the mercies of God, that you present your bodies a living sacrifice, holy, acceptable to God, which is your reasonable service.
>
> —Romans 12:1

Paul said to present your bodies a living sacrifice, holy and acceptable to God. Sacrifice hurts, so it's going to hurt that body to kill the deeds of the flesh. Verse 2 says, "And do not be conformed to this world, but be transformed by the renewing of your mind, that you may prove what is that good and acceptable and perfect will of God." This verse says that if you present your body, you can prove what is the good and acceptable and perfect will of God. Let the Word of God direct your body and your mind.

If you don't discipline your body, then it won't be disciplined. You need to temper yourself. All of that has to do with self-control and watching your behavior. You should be temperate, sober-minded, and of good behavior.

Ministers should not be having adulterous affairs on the side. There are so many that are involved in adultery and think that their church is okay.

Wives should not stand for that; they should not be so afraid that they are not going to be taken care of. Women, let me remind you that God is your source. Stand for righteousness, because the end of unholy and immoral living is not good. There are consequences to wrong choices. I know ministers that had affairs with woman after woman, even having children by these women, causing their wives to suffer, and the wife didn't have whatever it took to stand up and say, "I'm not living like this." God does not want you to be abused, misused, or run over. Trust your life to God. You have a place there by your husband's side, and he should honor that.

It is the husband's responsibility to give his wife her rightful place by his side. If he would give his wife her rightful place, there would not be so many women trying to get to him. There are many women who have tried to get to Apostle Price, but because of rules and boundaries he made for himself, their tricks have not worked.

There are more good women than bad. As a first lady, I wouldn't run a church without women. I love having women to come and help us do what God has called us to do. But many wives have so many fears and insecurities. If the pastor compliments another woman who looks good, they get upset and jealous. Well, he's not dead, and women are going to be looking good. It is OK for him to say other women look good and compliment them, as long as he compliments his wife and keeps her looking good. I don't mind Apostle Price complimenting other women because he takes excellent care of me. If he had not taken a stand about how he would relate to other women, he might not be where he is in ministry today, because the church was growing and the women came.

There was a woman who used to come to our Tuesday night Bible class. I saw how she dressed, wearing very low-cut, tight, and seductive clothing. She sat right across from me. I would always talk to her and was very friendly to her. Now, I never judged her for the way she dressed. I said, "Well, she is just out of the world, and she'll learn."I'm very naïve of heart, but I found out later that she was there for a purpose. One day she made an appointment with my husband. When he inquired as to what the appointment was about, she said to him, "I want you." Thank God he had made rules for himself. He stated that he said to himself, "My body says, 'I want you, too,' but my spirit says no!" He told her, "I can't help you," and opened the door and let her out. Ministers, this is what you have to do— make rules for yourselves and keep your spirit strong.

I had a woman in my Bible class come up to me and say that she had to leave the church because she could not stop lusting after Apostle Price. That did not upset me; I really wanted to help her.

Many women get it in their head that they are in love with the pastor or minister when in fact it is the anointing and the position that he holds that attracts them. A minister or pastor is very unwise for getting involved with a woman who pursues him. When the anointing is gone, his position is gone, and the church is gone, and she opens her eyes and sees that flesh, then it is a different story. When the minister gets involved with a woman who is after him, he becomes all messed up in his emotions and flesh, until he has no life left. I could tell you sad story after sad story of this happening. It's heartbreaking, and the collateral damage is incalculable.

There was a minister who had one of the largest churches in southern California. Some woman tempted him to get involved with her. He ended up leaving his church, which meant that he was without a position and an anointing. Then the woman left him, and he ended up messed up the rest of his life. I heard that he died alone in one of the southern states. Another minister left his wife for some young woman, and he ended up losing his church. Eventually, the woman left him sick and alone. How tragic, especially when it could have been avoided. So, men, you need to think about what you are getting into. The women are not going to hang around you once your power, anointing, and position are gone.

These stories are all true, and I could add others to these. My husband and I have seen many situations like this as we have traveled throughout the southern California area to minister. We have watched thriving churches fall apart and disappear into obscurity because of infidelity. I recall another minister in California who kept having affairs and finally got someone pregnant. He was taken to court, and it caused his wife a great deal of grief. She ended up getting sick and had to be placed in a special home, and then he ended up dying prematurely.

Young ministers, you can learn from some of these things that I am sharing and avoid the traps Satan will invariably set for you. These temptations are going to come your way, so you need to make rules and set boundaries for yourself. I cannot overemphasize that point. If I were you, I wouldn't want to be responsible for the death of a wife or many people rejecting or not accepting Jesus because I didn't live right. Many wives are not strong in God's Word and really don't know how to fight in the spirit, so they end up getting sick or dying prematurely. Do you want to be responsible for that?

CHAPTER 5

WHAT LEGACY WILL YOU LEAVE FOR YOUR CHILDREN?

PASTORS AND MINISTERS, WHAT KIND of example are you leaving your children when they see how you treat their mother?

Mothers and fathers are the first glimpse of God that children see. If they don't see God in you, many times it leaves them messed up. Many pastor's and minister's kids have said, "I don't ever want to see a church again." Your actions leave them confused, and oftentimes they go in directions that you later regret. I wouldn't want that on me. So think about it, ministers and men of God! Make rules and set boundaries for yourself. You can't have all of the women anyway, so you may as well love your wife and treat her as she ought to be treated. If you have a problem being faithful to your wife, you need to ask God to help you, because He said in Ephesians 5:25 to love your wife just as Christ loves the church. Christ would not abuse or misuse the church; neither should you abuse or misuse your wife.

If you will be an example for your children and live right before them, they will continue to serve in the ministry and stay in fellowship with God, because God will be real to them. The lives of many pastor's kids are messed up because their fathers and sometimes mothers did not live morally upright lives before them. Our children, our sons-in-law, and now even our grandchildren work in Fred's and my ministry. Our son, Pastor Fred Price Jr., was recently installed as pastor of Crenshaw Christian Center. I believe that is because we have lived lives of integrity and morally right before them; that is, a God-fearing life. Psalm 112:1–2 says, "Blessed is the man who fears the LORD, Who delights greatly in His commandments. His descendants will be mighty on earth; The generation of the upright will be blessed."

Ministers should live a life above reproach. Remember that God sees everything that you are doing. Make up your mind to do right by your children, do right by your church, do right by your ministry, and not take advantage of the spiritual sisters, the women that God has given to you as an under-shepherd. When you take advantage of them, you are defrauding them, and the Bible tells you to not defraud them. This also extends to you, sister so-and-so, who sets out to seduce and trap men in ministry. Don't be a spiritual black widow.

> For this is the will of God, your sanctification: that you should abstain from sexual immorality; that each of you should know how to possess his own vessel in sanctification and honor, not in passion

of lust, like the Gentiles who do not know God; that no one should take advantage of and defraud his brother in this matter, because the Lord is the avenger of all such, as we also forewarned you and testified. For God did not call us to uncleanness, but in holiness.

—1 THESSALONIANS 4:3–7

No Competition

Sometimes a husband and wife feel that they are both called to pastor. There should be no competition in ministry between husbands and wives. Sometimes wives get out of place and want to take the lead in ministry. Some even leave their husbands and sometimes leave their children, too, and start their own ministry. I believe that is out of order, because God would not call a wife to a ministry to neglect her first ministry, which is to her husband and children.

People will sometimes ask me, How does it make you feel being in the shadow of Apostle Price? I always respond that it makes me feel real good because it's a good shadow. I always share Psalm 91:1 with them about abiding under the shadow of the Almighty, which is a good shadow.

He who dwells in the secret place of the Most High
Shall abide under the shadow of the Almighty.

Also, Acts 5:15 says, "So that they brought the sick out into the streets and laid them on beds and couches, that at least the shadow of Peter passing by might fall on some of them." That was a good shadow. So we do not have to be afraid as women that we are going to be overlooked when we are under that good shadow.

We should be an example of a righteous God. We are representatives of Jesus Christ. How do we make Jesus look? Romans 6:11 says, "Likewise you also, reckon yourselves to be dead indeed to sin, but alive to God in Christ Jesus our Lord." That means to act like you are dead. The Bible says if your right hand or foot causes you to sin, cut it off.

> If your hand or foot causes you to sin, cut it off and cast it from you. It is better for you to enter into life lame or maimed, rather than having two hands or two feet, to be cast into the everlasting fire.
> —MATTHEW 18:8

If your body parts are causing you trouble, cut them off or act like they are dead, because if they are dead, you can't get into trouble. You who have problems in the flesh need to see yourself dead!

CHAPTER 6

SPIRITUAL PROSTITUTION

THERE IS SIN IN THE lives of ministers and lay people alike, but because God does not just wipe them out, apparently they think that they are getting away with their wrong living. Many are gifted and talented in the natural, and they know how to perform and entertain the people. Just as actors and actresses, they train themselves. But there is no anointing there, and God is not in what they are doing. As with the young lady who emailed me about the adulterous affair she was having with her bishop, she ministered, and even with sin in her life people were blessed; but she was miserable. Remember in Galatians 6:7–8, "Do not be deceived, God is not mocked; for whatever a man sows, that he will also reap. For he who sows to his flesh will of the flesh reap corruption." *Corruption* means "decay" and "dying." So if ministers continue in their immoral lifestyles, they are killing themselves. If you are in adultery, my prayer is that you will repent and glorify God in your spirit, soul, and body.

We need to be careful how we treat each other as a family because the church starts with the family. Many in ministry, men and women alike, and some missionaries, are good at conning, conniving, scheming, deceiving, and extorting. I call it spiritual prostitution. Many do and say things and have the ability to perform and to put a request out there as if they are helping the whole world and play on the emotions of people. People will give to them, and it's for these ministers' own greed. People need to be aware of this when someone is asking you to give to their churches and ministries. You need to look into whom you are giving to, into their background and their accomplishments, because you can give into bad ground.

My husband and I have been taken. I like to give, and whenever I hear of a need to help somebody or some caring ministry that is feeding the hungry or helping the poor, if it is within my reach, I like to be involved. Our ministry was giving to a ministry that was supposedly taking care of the poor and feeding the hungry. We found out later that they weren't right. We were so happy to be helping a ministry like that because every ministry is not called to or anointed to do everything that is needed in the body of Christ, so we were so blessed to support a ministry that was called to minister to the poor. We found out later that they were not using our seed rightly. You have to be careful whom you give to. Do not just give to a need, but find out what's behind that need.

God certainly wants you to give, because over and over in His Word He says to give to the poor. I am all for helping ministries and missions, but you better know whom you are helping. I heard a story about these young girls who were going to college in San Diego. They then decided to go to Tijuana. On the way, by the side of the road they saw a little dog, so they stopped and picked it up. It was hurt, in pain, and bleeding. They took him back to their apartment, washed him up, and put him in bed with them. They took him to the veterinarian and found out that he was not a cute little doggie but a rat from the region that was full of rabies. The girls ended up being infected. My point is, know whom you are giving to. I believe in giving, but you need to check to find out whom you are giving to.

CHAPTER 7

WARNING AGAINST COVETOUSNESS AND PRIDE

YOU DO NOT WANT TO be a covetous person. Ministers should not be covetous, but unfortunately there are a lot who are. *Covetousness* is defined as "an insatiable desire for gain," which could be gain for power, position, control, as well as money. Many people want power, and even if they don't have the money, some want control. They want the position. You have people in your church who want a certain position; they desire power. They want to be the greatest, they want to be the biggest—and they do not want anybody else to come along and be blessed.

I know of a minister who has the biggest problem with young ministers being blessed. Apostle Price and I have no problem with young ministers who are being blessed and are prospering, spirit, soul, body, materially, and financially. They should have more than we did when we were their age. They have been blessed to be able to put principles in operation in their early twenties, and we didn't learn of the principles until our late thirties. We are just happy that many of them are good students and have learned well and are now reaping the benefits at a young age.

There are nothing but blessings for those who walk uprightly.

> No good thing will He withhold From those who walk uprightly.
>
> —PSALM 84:11

Older ministers who have a problem with young ministers being blessed should read the story in the Bible about Saul and David. Saul could not stop David from being king. Ministers should rule their own houses well because Proverbs 20:7 teaches, "The righteous man walks in his integrity; His children are blessed after him." Ministers and pastors need to take care how they conduct themselves and obey what God has told them to do.

God's Word tells you everything you need to do to live a victorious, overcoming life. You should be victorious in your home as well as in the church. To me, it's a disgrace before God some of the stories I have heard about what men and women do in public and in their ministries that really affect the lives of people. Ministers should not think so much about what their flesh wants, yielding to the lust of their flesh. They should use God's Word to overcome the temptations of the flesh.

> Likewise you also, reckon yourselves to be dead indeed to sin, but alive to God in Christ Jesus our Lord. Therefore do not let sin reign in your mortal body, that you should obey it in its lusts. And do not

> present your members as instruments of unrigh-
> teousness to sin, but present yourselves to God as
> being alive from the dead, and your members as
> instruments of righteousness to God. For sin shall
> not have dominion over you, for you are not under
> law but under grace.
>
> —ROMANS 6:11–14

Many ministers and people are gifted in their delivery of God's Word. They can learn the principles of faith in their head. They can learn how to articulate it, they can learn how to preach it, they can learn how to demonstrate it, but it's not in their hearts. If it were in their hearts, they would not mistreat their wives, continue in adultery, and fail to be an example to their flocks or followers. If the Word of God were truly in the hearts of Christians, there would not be so much jealousy, envy, and strife. Many ministers, men and women, can preach the Word but have never repented of how they have treated other brothers and sisters in Christ, so God's Word remains in their heads. It cannot get into their hearts because of all the evil and junk that's there.

Many men and women seek praise and glory for themselves, and that is dangerous. That's something that Apostle Price has never allowed himself to do. All the things that we have ever done, we did to help people. We have never done anything for money or fame. We held television crusades for years across the United States and in Brisbane, Australia. My husband never received a dime for any of these times of ministry. He just wanted people to know the Word and get the truth. The ministry would pay his expenses, but he never received compensation for his ministry. He just wanted people to be set free as he was free, and through the Word of faith being ministered at these crusades, thousands upon thousands of people received salvation and got filled with the Holy Spirit. And many, many thousands of people have been set free as a result of the television ministry. Because of his desire to share God's Word, many ministers have said to him, "You are my spiritual father, you are my mentor." Their ministries have been blessed by him, and many have sown seed and continue to sow into his life, though we've never met them. My husband never ministered to get anything for himself, but because he has sown into the body of Christ, Christ takes care of him and always has. He is living proof that you do not have to scheme, deceive, connive, and do all kinds of junk to get money. God will take care of you if you do things right.

> Blessed is the man who fears the LORD, Who delights greatly in His commandments.... Wealth and riches will be in his house, And his righteousness endures forever.
>
> —PSALM 112:1, 3

> For our exhortation did not come from error or uncleanness, nor was it in deceit. But as we have been approved by God to be entrusted with the gospel, even so we speak, not as pleasing men, but God who tests our hearts. For neither at any time did we use flattering words, as you know, nor a

> cloak for covetousness—God is witness. Nor did
> we seek glory from men, either from you or from
> others, when we might have made demands as
> apostles of Christ.
>
> —1 THESSALONIANS 2:3–6

Ministers, I exhort you to use the words from the apostle Paul in not seeking glory from men. Ministers need to be continually committed to character. If a leader falls from these ethical standards, he or she should accept removal from leadership until an appropriate season of the re-verifying of their character can be fulfilled. So many ministers refuse to stop ministering when they have stepped out of character, so they are out there messing over God's people. They're still out there performing and using their talent to keep people coming, but there is no anointing on their ministry. This is pride.

If you have not taken time to be proven after you have fallen into sin and you have not taken the time to get that right, then you are just performing. There is no anointing on your life. People love to see a show, but you can do it God's way. You can decide to go to a true man of God and ask the man of God what you should do. When the man of God advises you according to the Word and you obey, asking God to forgive you, then God will restore your ministry to you. He will forgive you, but it takes time to be proven in ministry and to be restored, so that you can even prove to yourself that you can stand. But if you just keep on preaching after you have been involved in all kinds of sin and immoral living, you are just performing.

However, you can do what's right. Humble yourself and God will raise you up. You will feel so good because you're so clean inside. God washes you with the water of the Word. In 1 John 1:9, He says, "If we confess our sins, He is faithful and just to forgive us our sins and to cleanse us from all unrighteousness." We do not kill our wounded, as some people say the church does, but we tell them to get off of the battlefield until they get it together. Otherwise, they are going to get a lot of other people hurt. So think about this if you have fallen or know of others who have fallen and do not take the time to prove themselves. They are messing over their lives and others' lives as well.

Many years ago a young minister wanted Apostle Price to come to his church to minister. That young man's pastor heard about it and proceeded to inform my husband that this young minister was in adultery. So, of course, Apostle Price would not go minister at his church. The young minister immediately came to see my husband for counseling concerning his lifestyle, even though his pastor told him that he might not want to go to him because he was too hard or his rules were too rigid. The young minister said that he did not care because he had never seen a minister live a moral life. He had begun preaching as a young man, and all the ministers that he was around lived immoral lives. He asked Apostle Price what he should do. My husband told him to sit down from ministry for a year and allow his assistant minister to take care of the ministry, but still be in his church every week. He obeyed what Apostle Price told him to do. One year later, my husband restored him to his pulpit and his church has steadily grown. He has a wonderful wife and children and is being continually blessed.

Keep these words, ministers, and meditate on them.

> Let no one despise your youth, but be an example to the believers in word, in conduct, in love, in spirit, in faith, in purity. Till I come, give attention to reading, to exhortation, to doctrine. Do not neglect the gift that is in you, which was given to you by prophecy with the laying on of the hands of the eldership. Meditate on these things; give yourself entirely to them, that your progress may be evident to all. Take heed to yourself and to the doctrine. Continue in them, for in doing this you will save both yourself and those who hear you.
>
> —1 TIMOTHY 4:12–16

The Word of God should be thoroughly fastened in our hearts and minds concerning our ministries, and we must give our time and attention to its commandments. Because if we don't, we will just do the same old thing, and we will just act out of what's in our head. Matters of importance do not come automatically. You need to continue studying and meditating on the Word, praying in the spirit, building your spirit man up, and praying in the understanding so that you do not get complacent about the things of God. You need to take care of your spirit man, because if you do not, the soulish and fleshly man will take over. That is what happens to a lot of ministers. In Galatians 5:16, the Word says to "walk in

the Spirit, and you shall not fulfill the lust of the flesh."
The personal life of God's ministers ought to be as pure
as their doctrine or teaching. If the servant of the Lord
does not take heed to himself, his ministry will be mere
performance and acting with no anointing.

God's influence can depart from the human heart
through carelessness, and our minds can lose the inten-
sity of His call. Hebrews 2:1–3 states, "Therefore we must
give the more earnest heed to the things we have heard,
lest we drift away. For if the word spoken through angels
proved steadfast, and every transgression and disobedience received a just reward, how shall we escape if we
neglect so great a salvation, which at the first began to
be spoken by the Lord, and was confirmed to us by those
who heard Him." And it can happen. That's how people
get into sin. They stop spending time in the Word and
stop praying in the spirit, which would keep their spirit
strong. Then when temptation comes, they just go down
to the level of their flesh and yield to the temptation
because their spirit is not strong enough to ward it off.
When that happens, you can only go by what your mind
and body say.

Now may our God and Father Himself, and our
Lord Jesus Christ, direct our way to you. And may
the Lord make you increase and abound in love to
one another and to all, just as we do to you, so that
He may establish your hearts blameless in holiness

before our God and Father at the coming of our
Lord Jesus Christ with all His saints.

—1 THESSALONIANS 3:11–13

These verses are my prayer for you. First Thessalonians
4:1–8 tells us that we should abstain from sexual
immorality.

Finally then, brethren, we urge and exhort in the
Lord Jesus that you should abound more and more,
just as you received from us how you ought to walk
and to please God; for you know what commandments we gave you through the Lord Jesus. For
this is the will of God, your sanctification: that you
should abstain from sexual immorality; that each
of you should know how to possess his own vessel
in sanctification and honor, not in passion of lust,
like the Gentiles who do not know God; that no one
should take advantage of and defraud his brother in
this matter, because the Lord is the avenger of all
such, as we also forewarned you and testified. For
God did not call us to uncleanness, but in holiness.
Therefore he who rejects this does not reject man,
but God, who has also given us His Holy Spirit.

If you have problems abstaining, you should meditate
on and confess verse 3 until you are free from sexual
immorality. Verse 4 says we should know how to possess
our own vessel in sanctification and honor. God warns us
in all these verses and tells us that He is the avenger of
this kind of living. I suggest that all ministers and their
mistresses refrain from living this type of unholy and
unclean life because it will surely lead to death—death

of relationships with your spouses and children, the death of your ministry, or physical death. I pray that you will make boundaries for yourselves and stop sleeping around with someone whom you are not married to.

Man of God, when you think about messing over people's lives, you are messing up yourself, as well as your wife and your children, as well as the person that you are involved with, and perhaps your congregation. First Thessalonians 5:23 is also my prayer for you: "Now may the God of peace Himself sanctify you completely; and may your whole spirit, soul, and body be preserved blameless at the coming of our Lord Jesus Christ." I would like to leave these words with you, that as pastors and ministers of the gospel, you can live this life of holiness.

You do not have to fall into these types of temptations. Apostle Price and I have lived this life over fifty-five years. That's why you've never seen or heard of a scandal about Apostle Price. It is not that he is above this happening to him; rather, it's because he has made rules for himself and has set boundaries that he refuses to violate. Our lives are an open book. We are not one thing in public and something different in private. We can all live a life of obedience to God's Word and experience the peace of God, which passes all understanding. And as you live this wonderful life, you will be a continual blessing to others.

CHAPTER 8

EXCERPT FROM "AVOIDING THE SEX TRAP"

By Angela Evans

PASTORS, MINISTERS, BISHOPS, I BELIEVE there is a correlation between you and King David, based on the fact that you are powerful men within your spheres of influence.

Let's look at 2 Samuel 11:2–4:

> Then it happened one evening that David arose from his bed and walked on the roof of the king's house. And from the roof he saw a woman bathing, and the woman was very beautiful to behold. So David sent and inquired about the woman. And someone said, "Is this not Bathsheba, the daughter of Eliam, the wife of Uriah the Hittite?" Then David sent messengers, and took her.

He did that because he was the king, he was powerful, "and she came to him, and he lay with her, for she was cleansed from her impurity; and she returned to her house" (v. 4). What he and Bathsheba did was consensual. She could have run just like those whom many of you prey on.

Verse 5 explains, "The woman conceived; so she sent and told David, and said, 'I am with child.'" Now, David thinks, "Oh my, what are we going to do?" Because Uriah was in the army, he asked someone to bring Uriah to him. I think David hinted to Uriah that he should go home and spend some time with his wife. David's plan was that if Uriah would lay with his wife, then he could cover this up. "They'll think it's Uriah's baby, and everything will be fine," is probably what was going through David's head. For some reason, however, Uriah didn't do that, so David's final decision was to tell his man in charge to put Uriah on the front lines. That way he could be certain Uriah would be killed, and David could have Bathsheba—and that's what happened. That was not at all a good thing. Indeed, it was quite scandalous.

God sent the prophet Nathan to David, and here's what happened:

> Then the LORD sent Nathan to David. And he came to him, and said to him: "There were two men in one city, one rich and the other poor. The rich man had exceedingly many flocks and herds. But the poor man had nothing, except one little ewe lamb which he had bought and nourished; and it grew up together with him and with his children. It ate of his own food and drank from his own cup and lay in his bosom; and it was like a daughter to him. And a traveler came to the rich man, who refused to take from his own flock and from his own herd to prepare one for the wayfaring man who had come to him; but he took the poor man's lamb and prepared it for

the man who had come to him." [That's what you, pastor, minister, bishop, do when you take someone's wife.] So David's anger was greatly aroused against the man, and he said to Nathan, "As the LORD lives, the man who has done this shall surely die! And he shall restore fourfold for the lamb, because he did this thing and because he had no pity." Then Nathan said to David, "You are the man! Thus says the LORD God of Israel: 'I anointed you king over Israel, and I delivered you from the hand of Saul. I gave you your master's house and your master's wives into your keeping, and gave you the house of Israel and Judah. And if that had been too little, I also would have given you much more! Why have you despised the commandment of the LORD, to do evil in His sight? You have killed Uriah the Hittite with the sword; you have taken his wife to be your wife, and have killed him with the sword of the people of Ammon. Now therefore, the sword shall never depart from your house, because you have despised Me, and have taken the wife of Uriah the Hittite to be your wife.' Thus says the LORD: 'Behold, I will raise up adversity against you from your own house; and I will take your wives before your eyes and give them to your neighbor, and he shall lie with your wives in the sight of this sun. For you did it secretly, but I will do this thing before all Israel, before the sun.'"

—2 SAMUEL 12:1–12

Now when you talk about the causative and the permissive sense, God wasn't really going to cause this. David's sin is what opened the door for the adversity. And that's what you do, pastor, minister, and bishop, when you willfully sin in the face of God. Now, if you draw a parallel to David, man of God, you'll see it's not at all worth it.

I know of a situation going on right now where the husband has engaged in an extramarital relationship, has gotten a woman pregnant, and now the marriage of almost thirty-five years is over. He's now gone to live with the adulteress and their child. That is so sad. I also recently learned about another pastor who was married for twenty-nine years and has engaged in adultery. Now that marriage is over after almost thirty years. That's incredible!

You must be vigilant about not giving in to the temptation to commit sexual immorality and about maintaining proper boundaries. Think about what you're doing to your wives, to your children, to yourself, and to the people of God who've been entrusted to you. It is very, very hurtful and very devastating. I know of numerous stories about how these scenarios end. It's not a pretty picture. I don't believe that the adulterer can leave his wife, marry the adulteress, and they live happily ever after. The sword of adversity is going to be in their house.

I'm thinking of another story in which the people were married almost forty years and the man left his wife for a younger woman. He and his mistress had a child, and they were miserable for the rest of their lives. He finally passed away, but this son that they had was always in and out of jail the entire time they were married. They fussed and fought the entire marriage. That's a terrible existence.

See, I told you—you're not going to live happily ever after because you didn't get into that relationship the right way.

It's awful! Pastors, ministers, bishops, you need to know that you may be going through male menopause, also known as a mid-life crisis. Some survive the temptations and some don't! I just told you about a few who didn't.

Sometimes that woman who's after you just wants your stuff—your material possessions. She wants her car payment taken care of, she wants a nice place to live, because you and your wife have acquired a great deal after all of those years together. She sees all that you have, but once she's lured you away from your wife and your family, then you don't have anything anymore, especially if you live in a community property state, like California. Once you've been divested of everything you have and you're not as attractive to her anymore, she'll dump you. Once you've alienated your wife and humiliated your family, you will basically live lonely for the rest of your life. Don't do it men, don't do it!

Now, I'd like to go back to that parallel between King David and pastors, bishops, ministers, and the like. They say power corrupts, and absolute power corrupts absolutely. I think after acquiring all that power, David had just gotten a little beside himself.

Take a look at the following scriptures.

> For this reason I left you in Crete, that you should set in order the things that are lacking, and appoint elders in every city as I commanded you—if a man is blameless, the husband of one wife, having faithful children not accused of dissipation or insubordination. For a bishop must be blameless, as a steward of God, not self-willed, not quick-tempered, not given to wine, not violent, not greedy for money, but

hospitable, a lover of what is good, sober-minded, just, holy, self-controlled, holding fast the faithful word as he has been taught, that he may be able, by sound doctrine, both to exhort and convict those who contradict [or gainsayers].

—TITUS 1:5–9

"Woe to the shepherds who destroy and scatter the sheep of My pasture!" says the LORD. Therefore thus says the LORD God of Israel against the shepherds who feed My people: "You have scattered My flock, driven them away, and not attended to them. Behold, I will attend to you for the evil of your doings," says the LORD.

—JEREMIAH 23:1–2

That is scary!

Also I have seen a horrible thing in the prophets of Jerusalem [that could refer to men of God]: They commit adultery and walk in lies [because usually lies and adultery go together]; They also strengthen the hands of evildoers, So that no one turns back from his wickedness. [Pastor, that means you're a bad example.] All of them are like Sodom to Me, And her inhabitants like Gomorrah.

—JEREMIAH 23:14

This is a faithful saying: If a man desires the position of a bishop, he desires a good work. [The word for "bishop" in the Greek is *episkopos*, meaning "one who oversees a congregation, an overseer," or it could be a pastor or a priest.][1] A bishop then must be blameless, the husband of one wife [not of several mistresses], temperate ["temperate" is translated from *egkrates* in the Greek, and it means being self-controlled in appetite and so forth],[2] sober-minded [which is rendered *sophron* in the Greek and means "self-controlled as to opinion or passion, discreet"],[3] of good behavior [not misbehaving], hospitable, able to teach; not given to wine, not violent, not greedy for money, but gentle, not quarrelsome, not covetous; one who rules his own house well, having his children in submission with all reverence (for if a man does not know how to rule his own house, how will he take care of the church of God?); not a novice, lest being puffed up with pride he fall into the same condemnation as the devil. Moreover he must have a good testimony among those who are outside [in the community], lest he fall into reproach and the snare of the devil.

—1 TIMOTHY 3:1–7

Now, I have a question for you. If a pastor is supposed to rule his house well so he can take care of the church of God, how can he take care of the church of God if he's seducing every person he can get his hands on in the house of God? Pastors, if this is you, you're a little distracted, don't you think? You're supposed to be taking care of the house of God! You're taking care of them, all right. Woe unto you! It says in James 3:1, "My brethren, let not many of you become teachers, knowing that we shall receive a stricter judgment." Pastor, minister, bishop, you have a greater responsibility. This is not a game! Again, woe unto you! It's a matter of your will—a choice you make not to sin against God.

Now I want you to go back to 2 Samuel 11. We're going

to go back to the story of David. I want to do a little para-phrase, and I'm going to insert the word *pastors* in the scripture text.

> Then it happened one Sunday morning that when pastor ascended the pulpit, he walked around while he was ministering and saw the beautiful flowers (women) out in the congregation (v. 3). So the pastor sent and inquired about the women. Then the pastor sent ushers to take her to his office, where he went to meet her after the service (v. 4).

Let's move over to 2 Samuel 12:7–12. Pastor, bishop, you don't want this part of the story to be told to you. In the Bible, this is where Nathan is talking to David. In the paraphrase below, God is talking to you.

> I anointed you, pastor (v. 8). I gave you sheep to shep-herd. And if that had been too little, I also would have given you much more. Why have you despised the commandment of the Lord to do evil in His sight? You have taken his wife to be your wife and killed him with the sword—basically, you've killed someone's marriage. Now therefore the sword shall never depart from your house because you have despised me. Thus says the Lord, behold, I will raise up adversity against you. For you did it secretly, but I will do this thing before all (v. 12).

Wouldn't it be scary if this were what God had to tell you? I think there's a clear correlation between some pastors, ministers, and bishops and King David. Power is a heady thing, and some people can't handle it. Pastors, woe unto you for messing over those whom God has entrusted to you and those who belong to God. You are defrauding the people of God, which means you're violating and cheating them, and the Bible says not to do that.

Parishioners who stay in your church, where they know you, the pastor, are engaged in this kind of behavior, are aiding and abetting your crime. They know what you, as the pastor, are doing, and they still remain, still bring their tithes. That's not good ground. I know of two situations like this right here in my city. The members are telling me how disgusted they are with their pastors and what they're doing, so they're not going to church at all right now. You see, these pastors have scattered the sheep. This is very, very sad.

You, pastor, are going to pay a price for misleading these sheep.

Dr. Minnie Claiborne, a Christian therapist, said that as a counselor, she hears of horrible, detestable things happening among members of the clergy. Not only do so many of them have mistresses, but what is even more of an abomination is that many have *mister*-sses. Did you get that? How scary! That means they're on the down-low. Pastors, what are you giving to the people when you stand before them? I don't even know how you live with yourself.

First ladies should not stay there and sit on the front row like everything is all right when their husbands are engaged in this sin. You need to stay home or say, "I'm not going with you because you're a whoremonger, and

I'm not going to let the people think that you're OK." You affirm his behavior by being present.

Dr. Claiborne says the list of abominations that she hears about as a counselor include adultery, fornication, drug and alcohol addictions, homosexual relationships, and more. And the "more" includes pornography, which is destroying many men and their marriages—and these are men of God. Dr. Claiborne goes on to say that she often hears of accounts of women who have legitimate problems in their marriage and have gone to their pastor for counsel and he seduces them into sexual sin. Is that incredible?

Jesus says in Matthew 18:6, "Whoever causes one of these little ones who believe in Me to sin, it would be better for him if a millstone were hung around his neck, and he were drowned in the depth of the sea." Now the term *little ones* includes those who are vulnerable, as well as children. Did you know that "millstone" is *mulos* in the Greek? It referred to a large grinding stone that was so heavy that it needed to be turned by a donkey. Can you get a picture of that heavy stone around your neck? That means you're sinking to the bottom very quickly. Jesus is saying it would be better for you to be drowned in the ocean than to hurt one of these.

My hope is that pastors, ministers, and bishops, or any other person in positions of influence over sheep, will heed the warning that I have issued and turn away from their sinful way of life before it's too late. God has made a way of escape. You need only take it.

CHAPTER 9

DO YOU WANT TO BE FREE?

By Minnie Claiborne, PhD, LHD

I AM SO GRATEFUL TO GOD, to Dr. Betty Price, and to Mrs. Angela Evans for being bold enough to write this very needed and timely book. It should be a required text for every seminary and Bible school student and for everyone aspiring to the ministry.

As a Christian counselor I have heard many of the horrible stories of abuse, lust, perversion, and destruction caused by men who have occupied the trusted office of pastor or the position of minister. Like Dr. Betty, I have counseled many of their devastated victims.

I have met the mistresses who are in criminal, abusive relationships with married ministers and are too trapped and afraid to get out. I've met the ones who have angry and confused children who keep silent for various reasons. I've counseled husbands whose wives became victims of prey when they sought counseling from their pastor, whom they supported and trusted. This is so sad.*

---

* A small percentage of molestations are perpetrated by women. Their punishment should be no less severe. However, the overwhelming number of atrocities are committed by men.

Both men and women whom I have counseled have been molested by men who call themselves ministers or bishops. Some of these were molested by their own fathers! I'm speaking of men and women who were molested as children by their natural fathers who hold offices of pastor and bishop. I've counseled young men who were raped, seduced, or molested by homosexual pastors. I know pastors who are drug addicts; child molesters; homosexuals; adulterers; fornicators; spousal abusers emotionally, mentally, financially, and physically; men who twist the scriptures in order to justify their sinful behaviors. According to Dr. Ted Roberts, president of Pure Desire Ministries, 65 percent of pastors in America are addicted to pornography. Wait, this sounds exactly like the list of people whom the Bible says "will not inherit the kingdom of God" (Gal. 5:19–21).

Dr. Loren Due, son of a prominent Pentecostal minister and author of *Shhh... Don't Say a Word About This: Exposing Sin and Confronting Sexual Perversion*, overcame incest, rape, sexual abuse, and molestation through a process of therapy, prayer, and the Word of God. Dr. Due says, "I have concern for those who claim to be my brothers and sisters in Christ, yet insist that homosexual behavior is fine and natural! I fear for them, just as I do for those who are committing adultery, who are full of pride or who are greedy and selfish. When we are doing the things that God is against and making excuses for it, we are in deep trouble."[1] Dr. Due references Romans 1:26–27 which calls homosexuality and lesbianism "vile" and "unseemly."

Recently, *Ladies' Home Journal* magazine featured an article entitled "Behind Closed Doors." In it, they cited an FBI report that found doctors, educators, police, and clergymen have all been prosecuted for Internet child pornography. The article explained, "A congressionally funded study found that almost all of those arrested for possessing child porn were men."[2] Many sexual predators are using the Internet. This has led to the increase of the instances of repeated child molestation.

We know that the problem exists; the sad aspect is that it is prevalent among "the saints." Even sadder is the fact that the church does not want to even talk about it, much less deal with it. Whether these men are actually ministers of Satan, disguised as angels of light, or sin-possessed, so-called men of God who are in danger of being castaways, the destruction and devastation is overwhelming and must be confronted. Second Corinthians 11:13–15 reads, "For such are false apostles, deceitful workers, transforming themselves into apostles of Christ. And no wonder! For Satan himself transforms himself into an angel of light. Therefore it is no great thing if his ministers also transform themselves into ministers of righteousness, whose end will be according to their works."

I believe that God has prompted Dr. Betty and Angela Evans, as he has me, to insist that we confront these issues and the guilty parties and to provide help for those who are true victims and sincerely want to change.

Why Do They Do It?

There are two basic motivations for sin:

1. Willful sinning—blatant and arrogant sin and disobedience to God; no fear of God; lust; an undisciplined lifestyle; no intimate, personal relationship with the Lord Jesus Christ;

2. Untreated victimization—an individual was abused in some way or experienced some type of trauma and never received proper help.

In both cases, Christians are without excuse and must not continue in the sin. This is why Jesus Christ lived a sinless, sacrificial life, surrendered to death on a cross, and arose with all power. And, if you are reading this book, you have been given proper warning and steps to recovery if you want help.

For those who are willfully sinning and have no fear of God, or who are mistaking God's longsuffering as His endorsement or "permissive will" over your lifestyle, you are sadly mistaken. Your position, money, education, or anointing do not exempt you from God's judgment and wrath. You are not in God's perfect, or decreed, will. God permits or allows everything that man does, but He does not cause you to sin. You are in willful sin and disobedience, and you are hurting other people whom God loves and for whom Jesus gave His life. Galatians 6:7 warns, "Be not deceived, God is not mocked, for whatever a man sows, that will he also reap." There are many biblical and current-day examples of this. If you persist in willfully and continually sinning against God and His people and making a mockery of the ministerial office, your end has already been determined.

Jesus said in Matthew 7:21–23, "Not everyone who says to Me, 'Lord, Lord,' shall enter the kingdom of heaven, but he who does the will of My Father in heaven. Many will say to Me in that day, 'Lord, Lord, have we not prophesied in Your name, cast out demons in Your name, and done many wonders in Your name?' And then I will declare to them, 'I never knew you; depart from Me, you who practice lawlessness [wickedness]!'" The voice of the "many" in this scripture sounds exactly the way preachers talk. Jesus is talking specifically about preachers here!

The apostle Paul said, "But I discipline my body and bring it into subjection, lest, when I have preached to others, I myself should become disqualified" (1 Cor. 9:27). Another version reads "lest...I myself should be a castaway" (KJV). I do not write this as someone who is perfect or has already attained. I have made mistakes, as we all have, but I do not embrace or live a sinful lifestyle or exploit and abuse those to whom God has called me to minister.

If you choose to repent and move forward with God sincerely, He will surely help you. Repentance does not just mean you're sorry. Dr. LaVerne Tolbert, author of *Keeping You and Your Kids Sexually Pure* says, "If you're only sorry for your sins, even really, really sorry; without true, Godly repentance you won't stop sinning."[3] This fact is clearly confirmed by the woman who wrote the second letter reproduced in chapter 1 of this book. She quotes the bishop she is having an affair with as saying, "Oftentimes I ask the bishop, Aren't you afraid of the Lord, or do you and He have just that tight understanding? He says that every time he leaves my presence, he feels really bad, but not bad enough to just stop."

Nine Steps to Freedom from Sexual Sin

The following list presents eight of Dr. Tolbert's nine steps of true repentance, which are brilliantly outlined in *Keeping You and Your Kids Sexually Pure* and are available on her Web site, www.teachinglikejesus.org.

1. Agree with God that what He calls sin, is sin.

2. Admit to God that your lifestyle is sin and that it violates His Word.

3. Acknowledge that you are powerless to stop your behavior.

4. Admit that you may not even want to change your behavior.

5. Accept God's chastisement and know that you are a child whom He loves.

6. Accept His forgiveness and cleansing and refuse feelings of guilt and condemnation.

7. Appropriate God's Word to help you when tempted, by memorizing Scripture, repeating it often, and doing what the Bible says.

8. Accountability, either to a small group or to one or two friends you can trust provides a safe place of sharing, prayer, and repentance.[4]

Help if You Feel Trapped and Want to Get Out

One of the women who wrote to Dr. Betty described an abusive, controlling, and dangerous relationship: "He got angry, and I got scared. So, we are in a relationship still. He ended up saying that God wanted me to be a good girl and to stop giving him trouble. If I do what God wants, then all my ministries would come forth. Right now, he says I am hindering the work of the Lord by being this way to him." The legal term for this is *domestic violence* or *domestic abuse.* He does not have to be living with you in order for it to be domestic abuse. According to FBI and police reports and the National Center for Domestic Violence, the definition of *abuse* is as follows:

The terms "Domestic Violence," "Domestic Abuse" and "Battering" are generally used interchangeably. They all refer to the increasingly severe pattern of verbal, emotional, psychological, physical, and sexual abuse for the purpose of intimidation; instilling fear and controlling another person's life and behavior.

The term "domestic" may imply that the abuse

must occur in the home or that it must be perpetrated by a husband or live-in partner. Actually domestic abuse is abuse that is perpetrated by any person against another with whom an intimate relationship has been established. This includes boyfriends, ex-boyfriends, husbands, ex-husbands, or someone with whom a woman has had a child.

The general public and many women think that a woman must be slapped, punched, kicked, stabbed, or shot—in other words, extremely physically hurt—before serious domestic violence or abuse has occurred.

However, domestic violence consists of other behaviors that are just as destructive, and which are also illegal. Many women say that the mental and emotional abuse is worse than the physical abuse.

The behaviors include:

- Constant criticism
- Degrading and demeaning language
- Cursing
- Throwing things
- Breaking things
- Name-calling
- Threatening
- Put-downs
- Controlling the person's time or money
- Restraining her against her will
- Threats of harm
- Unwanted sexual acts

- Telephone harassment
- Stalking
- Threatening friends or family members

These acts are crimes punishable by law.

The "Jekyll and Hyde" Personality

Abusers are said to have a "Jekyll and Hyde" personality. They may be loving, kind, caring, and charming one minute and violent, angry, cruel, and abusive the next. When it comes on, it's like a water hose without a shut-off valve.

The woman in this type of relationship walks around on eggshells. She tries to constantly adjust her behavior so that she doesn't make him angry. She doesn't realize that he is just an angry, sick person. It has nothing to do with her. No matter what she does, the cycle or pattern of abuse is part and parcel of his behavior.

Friends and family usually don't witness the abuser's rage. That's one of the reasons it's referred to as domestic abuse. The abusive behavior usually occurs behind closed doors in the home. The abuser may be charming, helpful, and gregarious around others, but he turns into a cruel, raging, out-of-control monster in private.

Research shows that abusers dehumanize their victims in their minds, thereby showing no empathy for the person upon whom they inflict pain. If he views her as his property, his possession, to use and control as he sees fit, he sees no need to love, respect, or care for her. Her victimization, learned helplessness, and codependency reinforces his sense of being powerful.

Lethality Checklist

Some abusers are extremely dangerous and are more likely to kill their partners. The following are indicators of this level of severity:

- Threats of homicide or suicide
- Fantasies of homicide or suicide
- Depression
- Weapons
- Obsessive about partner or family
- Centrality of the abused woman
- Rage
- Drug or alcohol consumption

How to Escape: Breaking the Soul Tie

Have you heard the term *soul tie*? Your soul is comprised of your mind, will, and emotions. All three components are intertwined with another person's when you become seriously involved with them. Additionally, when the relationship includes sex, you have joined together on another level. God intended this to happen in God-ordained marriages. But don't forget the evil spirits that are involved in sinful acts, such as fornication, adultery, and homosexuality, which are outside of the marriage covenant as God defines it. This kind of bond has serious consequences. These are just some of the reasons that it is sometimes very hard to just break off such relationships, even when they are harmful and miserable. One of the women who wrote to Dr. Betty mentioned suicide; she does not know how to escape her misery.

You've probably heard the saying, "Sin will take you further than you ever intended to go, keep you longer than you intended to stay, and cost you more than you intended to pay." But thank God for His great love for us. There is a way out! Read these loving words from the Book of Hebrews 2:16–18 (RSV):

> For surely it is not with angels that he is concerned but with the descendants of Abraham. Therefore he had to be made like his brethren in every respect, so that he might become a merciful and faithful high priest in the service of God, to make expiation for the sins of the people. For because he himself has suffered and been tempted, he is able to help those who are tempted.

You and I who believe in Jesus Christ are, by faith, also descendants of Abraham. God is concerned about us. He is merciful and faithful and will help us when we come to Him humbly and honestly.

> That is why it depends on faith, in order that the promise may rest on grace and be guaranteed to all his descendants—not only to the adherents of the law but also to those who share the faith of Abraham, for he is the father of us all.
>
> —ROMANS 4:16, RSV

Do your spiritual prayer work first. Then you will have the strength to follow through in the natural/practical.

Seven Steps to Victory

1. Repent to God and truly ask for His forgiveness. Psalm 51 is a good one to pray. In that psalm, David states that God desires truth. Be honest with God about your fears, your feelings, your desires—everything. Ask for His help. Review Dr. Tolbert's nine steps of repentance.

2. Set aside an hour or so daily so that you can talk to God, praise and worship Him, read His Word, and be still in His presence. This will allow you to hear any direction or encouragement that He may speak to your spirit.

3. Once you have established intimacy with God, ask Him to help you break the soul tie, the emotional, mental, and spiritual entanglement with the person with whom you were or are having a sinful relationship.

4. Read the entire book of Ephesians aloud. Read and meditate on other scriptures that affirm who you are in Christ.

5. If you have someone who is spiritually mature whom you can trust, ask him or

her to be your prayer partner and accountability partner. For females, an older woman
is usually better.

6. Ask God for wisdom. Choose the time,
place, and method in which you will tell the
other party that the game is over.

7. Continue your intimate time with God;
change churches if the individual with
whom you have been having the inappropriate relationship attends or is in
leadership there; get good, professional
Christian counseling; and fortify yourself
with scriptures and a good support system.
You must do the work. Faith without works
(actions) is dead. Do whatever you need to
in order to avoid contact with the person.
It's not worth losing your eternal soul or
your mind.

If you are in an abusive situation and fear retaliation,
call the National Domestic Violence Hotline. They are
available twenty-four hours a day at 1-800-799-SAFE.
They speak one hundred languages. You may also have to
call the police and seek a restraining order.

Help for Unmet Emotional Needs
and Emotional Traumas

One of the mistresses quoted previously in this book wrote to Dr. Betty saying that she has low self-esteem. She mentioned an incident that left her feeling rejected and perhaps contributed to her vulnerability. The other woman mentioned that she had become promiscuous in her efforts to ease her pain and break off her sinful relationship. By doing this, she is only making matters worse, creating more soul ties and sinking deeper into sin.

Ladies, if you are in a relationship with a married pastor, minister, or bishop, until you use the advice that we have given and submit to God and resist the devil, Satan will not flee from you. You're expecting the man of God to stop. He apparently won't. Don't be fooled by his "anointing." Consider what Jesus says in Matthew 7:21–23.

I realize that some people are vulnerable due to events in their pasts that created wounds that have never been healed or resolved. God has provided help. If you've ever experienced rejection, abandonment, molestation, rape, low self-esteem, and such, you are vulnerable and need to be healed. I have spent the past twenty years of my life helping people to be healed from such traumas and to move forward into God's glorious purpose and destiny for their lives. My book, *Prayer Therapy: Stop Hurting*, outlines God's simple solutions to complex problems. It is also available as a powerful audio book. All are available on my Web site, www.drminnie.net. Remember, God's plans for you are good and not evil, to give you a future and a hope. (See Jeremiah 29:11.)

Notes

Chapter 8
Excerpt from "Avoiding the Sex Trap"

1. *Strong's Exhaustive Concordance* (Dugan Publishers, Inc.), s.v. "episkopos."

2. Ibid., s.v. "egkrates."

3. Ibid., s.v. "sophron."

Chapter 9
Do You Want to Be Free?

1. Dr. Loren Due, *Shhh...Don't Say a Word About This: Exposing Sin and Confronting Sexual Perversion*, www.drdue.net.

2. Jan Goodwin, "Behind Closed Doors," *Ladies' Home Journal* (November 2008), http://www.lhj.com/relation-ships/family/safety/behind-closed-doors-child-pornog-raphy/ (accessed March 24, 2009).

3. Dr. LaVerne Tolbert, *Keeping You and Your Kids Sexually Pure* (Philadelphia, PA: Xlibris, 2009).

4. Ibid., 79.

More Books by
Dr. Betty R. Price

Wisdom From Above, Volumes 1 and 2

Says Dr. Betty, "This book has been written with the aim to help believers, especially women, know their rights in Christ, to encourage them to reach for the highest call of God, and to live the victorious, overcoming life."
Vol. 1 ISBN: 978-1-59979-241-5
Vol. 2 ISBN: 978-1-59979-382-5

Through the Fire & Through the Water
My Triumph Over Cancer

In 1990, Dr. Betty laid in her hospital bed under a possible sentence of death when she heard words of life in her spirit: "This illness is not unto death, but that the Son of God may be glorified through it." Dr. Betty and the Price family share the story of her battle.
ISBN: 978-1-883798-33-8
(Also available in Spanish and audiobook)

Lifestyles of the Rich & Faithful

In this book Dr. Betty candidly explores the challenges faced by many Christians today in handling perplexing problems that are hindering them from receiving the promised blessings of God.
ISBN: 978-1-883798-40-6

Standing by God's Man

It definitely takes a lot of grace—God's grace—not only to be a Christian wife, but also to be a preacher's wife. This book offers Dr. Betty's testimony of her early years and is a recipe to supporting and living with a great man of God.
ISBN: 978-1-883798-49-9

For the latest information on other books, visual, and audio products please contact us at (800) 927-3436. **www.faithdome.org**

Most Recent Audio Releases by Dr. Betty R. Price

Six Ways to Transform Your Life

The life of the believer should be one of constant growth, marked by goodness, righteousness, and truth. These teachings will help the believer to mature in God's Word and live a life that is far greater than mere existence.

BPD 18 (6-CD)

Wisdom From Above

These six teachings by Dr. Betty specifically speak to the issues that plague so many Christian women and describe how to overcome these difficulties through God's Word. This wealth of wisdom includes such teachings as "What's On Your Mind?" "Making Wise Choices," "How to Deal With Your Issues," and much more.

BPD 8 (6-CD)

Healing Is Our Covenant Right

Is it God's will for Christians to suffer in sickness and disease? Your church may say it is, but what does God's Word say about this matter? Learn the truth about your covenant right to healing and divine health, and then live well!

BPT 1 (4-CD)

A Lifestyle of Excellence

Having God's best is a process of operating in faith and walking in a godly lifestyle. If you want to know what is keeping you from receiving God's blessings, you need this series to give you the tools to walk in God's prosperity in spirit, soul, and body.

BPT 3 (4-CD)

For the latest information on other books, visual, and audio products please contact us at (800) 927-3436.

www.faithdome.org

Holy Living for Godly Women

In these two moving, eye-opening teachings, Dr. Betty Price speaks boldly about different situations women of God find themselves falling into when they do not obey God's Word and directive for their lives. Citing real-life examples, Dr. Betty shares profoundly about how loneliness can lead women into having children out of wedlock, living with men outside of marriage, adulterous affairs—and the consequences that ultimately follow these decisions. Dr. Betty also speaks frankly about abusive situations married women and their children can find themselves in, and the disastrous results that could last throughout the rest of their lives.

On the other hand, Dr. Betty cites real-life examples of how tending to the work of the Lord and diligently walking in His Word will lead to blessings beyond anything you could ever ask or imagine—such as receiving a mate, healing, and prosperity—and the peace of God that inevitably follows after believing God and acting on His promises.

Women of God, let these teachings transform your life into the godly living that your heavenly Father intended for you.

BPT9D (2-CD)